THE NAMELESS PLACES

Richard Lambert

THE NAMELESS PLACES

ARC
PUBLICATIONS
2017

Published by Arc Publications,
Nanholme Mill, Shaw Wood Road
Todmorden OL14 6DA, UK
www.arcpublications.co.uk

978 1911469 00 1 (pbk)
978 1911469 01 8 (hbk)
978 1911469 02 5 (ebk)

Design by Tony Ward

ACKNOWLEDGEMENTS
The author is grateful to the editors of the following
publications where some of the poems were published: *PN
Review*, *Poetry Ireland Review*, *Poetry Review*, *The Rialto*, *The
Spectator*, the *Times Literary Supplement*, and *The Yellow Nib*.
His thanks go to Arts Council England for their support
through a Grant for the Arts.
Thanks are also due to: the members of Norwich Stanza,
particularly Julia Webb, Stuart Charlesworth, Sally Festing,
Ramona Herdman, Peter Wallis, and Lynn Woollacott;
Moniza Alvi for reading the manuscript; and Jo Guthrie,
Laura Scott, and Heidi Williamson for their editorial
judgement, friendship, and advice.

Cover image:
'Middle Road East' by Katarzyna Coleman
(acrylic & charcoal on canvas, 2016),
by kind permission of the artist.

Editor for the UK & Ireland
John Wedgwood Clarke

CONTENTS

1. The Rebel Angel

On the wall there's a silhouette
you find is just a shadow from the trees
because the opera house is empty now, of course,
and in the square the rebel forces have long dispersed
though a solitary angel hangs from a lamp-post, dressed
in tar and feathers. He's fifty, fat,
and broken in half like this sonnet.

2. The Library

The library is empty now, of course, but you notice
how its fan design is based upon an Alexandrian
notion of extent, since taken up by the Venetians,
sundry *bibliothèques*, private archives, but here grotesque

what with the angel hanged in the broken window
or should I say apsidal light, what with the way
he keeps singing while the card index plays
with the unfixability of the word 'shadow'

which might easily apply to this desk
where the shade of his body keeps swinging
though if that is the result of his singing
or the wind through the broken window, grotesque

as it is, the card index will not tell,
being scattered now, an alphabet of hell.

3. The Theologian

The big-brained theologian who dragged
two scribes to trace his flood of thought, his memory
larger than Apulia, trained in exegesis,
wrestler with the mystic-rational nexus, Prof.,
polemicist who required armed guards
on bitter lecture days (Paris, Left Bank, '71),
taker-on of hundreds in quodlibetal disputation,
black-gowned, God's dog, eminently assailable,
with volutes of green leaf beginning to unfurl,
took a break in speech. One scribe
flexed, unflexed, his fist. The other yawned.
The Bible, with its big words, paused. Air poured.

4. THE REBEL ANGELS

But leaning on their forearms, their wings
unhooked and hung on chairs
among mirrors, rails and mannequins,
their baroque, implacable boredom in the air,
who, or what, are they waiting for?

Through deeper alleys, plazas, lanes
the rebel angels roam, seeking doors, an upper room,
a floor on which to sleep,
dispersed, their futures lost –
while clouds stream across the roofs like refugees.

5. The City and the River

All the city's emendations and asseverations
– the plot of waste, the disused offices,
the overflow, the unspooled tapes – ,
the river takes her slow lope round, tracing
a strangeness that the city does not deny,
the river examining them, letting them go by.

6. The Sluice

> Towards dusk the river
> packs volume between narrow banks, and slows –
> purple-pink cloud, shadowed houses –
> the river approaches the sluice.

> And this building of frosted glass,
> as dead as an abandoned swimming pool,
> welcomes the horse-powered force
> with dynamos, gauges, needle-verve, and the river
> vanishes.

> There is a sound
> that rumbles, flaps like flames in air, thunders
> in continuous reverberation underground
> before, jumbling chutes of white, tips juiced
> a lucent green, the river fans beneath the night.

7. THE BRIDGE AT NIGHT

Its arch shimmers with reflected moon
for part of the month, is dark the rest,
its pointing furred with moss. And when
a rowboat enters, it wakes into oar-booms
at such a sudden, unexpected guest.
From outside it seems a perfect circle
of darkness, half night air,
half the river's black. Oars
thud in the runnels. There's a trickle
from a mysterious pipe. It's the old miracle
of weight-bearing bricks that will crumble,
its depths filled with what's dropped off the top –
wrappers, coins, heavy sacks. They tumble
into a depth of weeds that winter stops.

8. The Outskirts

At some point the city gives up and goes away
though you couldn't say precisely where or why.
Perhaps it's at the bridge over the motorway
though it's not really, it's more in the mood
of the buildings, half-hidden behind trees, disused,
and sheets of newspaper cartwheeling to mishap
in the long grass by second-hand dealerships
at this border where people are only moving through,
never from or to. Unless they live here, of course,
which in a way we do, although there isn't a human
soul in sight, only, in this field a piebald horse
tied by a wet rope to the heart of dawn
all the way through to night and the night's damp,
illuminated faintly, last time you looked, by a streetlamp.

1. The Station Hotel

Down in the deep street a horse
has unchained itself from your dream
and stands by the station entrance
where no trains arrive or leave any more.

*

In the lobby you can fill in the spaces yourself
the way the hotel detective has filled in the newspaper
crossword, and left it on the arm of his deep chair.

*

It's not just the hotel that's empty, of course,
but the city, surrounded by a six-lane orbital
of yellow-eyed vehicles that hum through the walls.

*

Dining alone in the restaurant, at a noise
you put down your knife and fork and turn
but no-one is there except, in the mirror,
a man with no face, which is yours.

2. A Late Guest

The way her suitcase weighed her down,
I wondered what it held.
Her hands, when she signed the register,
were smooth, the veins as blue
as china, the bone at each temple
as delicate as china too. And her eyes,
when she lifted them to mine, were strange,
one green, one blue. Which is when she raised
an index finger, its pad inked black
like a fingerprinted criminal's, and said,
It leaks. And it did,
the fountain pen had blotted
her name. It was only afterwards
– after I had offered her a handkerchief
and she replied, *Don't worry about it* –
after she had gone,
that I thought it was deliberate, her spill,
after she had vanished entirely,
not even checking out, leaving
her suitcase on the bed which,
when opened,
contained a life, neither alive nor dead.

3. The Hotel Pool

He does not stop. I wonder what it is
that draws him to the pool, makes water his,
and once he's gone, wrapped in a towel,
once he's abandoned his cage-like prowl,
his watery pilgrimage, I wonder – can he sleep?
Because something more is keeping him
going to these lengths than exercise –
some thought or dream he might surprise
by following it through the pale blue light.

Although what he traces I can't know
in the gloom, in the slap and the slow
rhythm of his legs and arms breaking
the surface. At each end's flip, light flaking,
does he see wonders? Renounce all splendour?
Who or what is it that he tenders
to the pool? Now he hangs by the wall
in a funny, jellyfish sprawl,
now assumes his weight as he climbs
the ladder to his self, his time.

4. The Maid

With its deep, swirling carpets and uplit walls,
its wooden staircase and the metal *whsk*
of the lift's concertina doors,
slowly the hotel stirs.

The guests appear in ones and twos,
scented by aftershave, seaweed shampoos,
but drifting slowly, as ghosts might.

I strip the beds
possessed of each room's staleness, dust,
UHT milk tubs, empty coffee cups,
nostril hairs on pillowslips,
wrinkled tissues in a bin,
blood stains on bed linen.

In one guest's tidy, rumpled room
I touch a woman's cardigan,
lift her lipstick, carmine red,
beside a note to self – *scarf for S.*
I leave the room almost as it was.

In one, I open windows.
The muslin curtain blows.

At night, upon my narrow bed
beneath the rafters, on the wall
I see a picture of a lake.
Under moonlight, clouds, or rain,
across the city's
mansard roofs and gable ends.

I sift the grainy light of dawn, and weigh
what's taken and what's left.

5. The Union Hotel Carol

Nights in the union hotel
the ammonite
nights in the union hotel
your white hands
nights in the union hotel
the laundry room in darkness
nights in the union hotel
the laundry bags piled high

Nights in the union hotel
it's time to dance
nights in the union hotel
a word to the wise
nights in the union hotel
a chandelier trembles
nights in the union hotel
the door is wide

Nights in the union hotel
the guests are sleeping
nights in the union hotel
the pillow burns
nights in the union hotel
the empty ballroom
nights in the union hotel
someone cries

6. The Green Fish

The city was placed here just so,
a picture where no-one appears.

It would be better to leave it
as clear as the moon

shining in the top left corner
of the window

but there's a bright green fish the size of a carp
in your arms, and it's this bright green fish,

its yellow eye, its grin,
that's the poem. You sit on a chair

in the hotel room, with the bright green fish
across your arms like a dog or a child

or the long hair of a girl kneeling in grief
whom you want to console, and the moon looks in

at the picture window,
and the sky turns green, pink, rose.

POEM OF THE HAND

small crumpled animal
of sleep

    *

moves like a spider

    *

for nearly seven hours
no-one injured it

    *

The dead hand of the wind
The dead hand of the wind

    *

could fit inside the moon

SLIGHT POEM ON A ROUGH SURFACE

so much sleight
on the surface seems

salient: it will take a while
to work it out

*

so much slight
lament

      underneath

the wire gods – tiny claws
on clawed rods –

       The mouse
in the machine!

UNNECESSARY POEM

Like the engine hoisted from the body of a car
and laid on trestles –
Beautiful, but it won't work.

1. To the Far Moon

It's true that the hedgehog is bundled in leaves
    and the swans have flown over the water.
You're faint as a glimmering stone in the stream
    or the scar on a friend's lovely arm;
you've gone all the way to the end of the sky –
    when are you coming home?

2. Harvest Moon

The moon lives at the end of the fields,
curled in a hollow, covered with leaves
and swollen from summer. Careful, or she'll startle
awake. I swear I heard her breathe.

3. Lullaby of the Moon

It's a murmuring of language that you don't understand.
Out past nodding masts to her track upon the sea
where octopus and sea anemone pretend to listen in –
they're deaf, of course, and under ocean tonnes,
so they don't hear a thing. But the sea otters do,
wet and sleek upon their stones, quick and still;
they hear through the wind-muffled waves
just like you, whose open shutter lets her in
so she sings her human songs.

4. In her Last Scene…

The moon comes to the big window and leans, like one of those old movie stars. Pretty soon she's pushed her shoulder off the frame and is small where a moment ago she seemed to fill the whole room. She moves slowly (it's the end of the movie and she's tired), trailing her long, white chiffon robe until she's obscured by the pines. Opening the window, then stepping into the garden where everything's bathed in her strange, pale glow, you're overcome by how distinct and tiny she is, and overcome by how your own biography pervades everything, even the garden, even her shape in the sky, even this, these poems trying to become real.

5. Little Romance of the Moon

1. *Haunts*

The moon takes a room in Paris
with wallpaper of *fleur-de-lys*
where the mirror's fluorescent tube
makes her look ill and old.

She goes to the haunts she used to,
in a mirror meets some boy's glance
but when his interest drifts,
it makes her feel old and ill.

2. *Fame*

When they put her name up in lights,
in pink and blue neon tubes,
she'll have her work cut out, getting home
through streets that have gone entirely dark.

3. *Dawn*

The moon enchants by being new,
the moon enchants by being true;
neither now, she moves
slowly through the morning blue.

SUMMER NIGHT

The stars whose light left aeons ago
wink in the sky as if turning on threads

and the earth, warm from the heat of the sun,
sleeps like an old man in a house, his face

wrinkled and cracked, his eyes closed with sand,
and the houses' volumes under the trees

sleep too, as if they themselves
were the sleepers they held.

THE DEER

In the summer fields your life left you.
She ran out from under the hood of your heart
and tottered across the tarmac on clippy-cloppy hoofs
like a teenage girl in heels.

No time to notice the evening light,
the sun low down on the green high crops,
only time to brake and watch
her go one way then the other, unsure

at the sight of your wide, loud car –
alien, yes, off-white and wild; you glimpsed her
on a patch of burned waste ground
that must have been scorched for a reason, and passed.

A COUNTRY VISITOR

Smudge, smoke, a faint layer
of soot, the tang
of burned wood on the tongue –
you are here all afternoon, lingering
over the hot fields, scorched ground.

You appear without a sound,
the knot of your tie crooked,
your change loose;
the sweatband of your bowler
leaves a crease through oiled hair.

By the fork at the woods
you slip the noose, offering
to take us with you just this once,
and when you're gone I wonder if
I made you up, a shadow I

could lift and hang
like a suit.

They grow, these nubs.
Bulbs of hardened skin,
then buds, humps.
Then a branch, a single one,
so I believed myself
a tree before a second
crowned me king,
two candelabra, excrescences
hard as wood, my mouth
immobile, my face
regally stiff.

Who made me like this,
my thoughts bright ingots,
nuclear rods, my antlers
cold as stone? Which boundary
did I cross? Which god
did I offend?

I am like Job
in that I curse God.
I do.
I curse God.

Just to put it straight,
so there is no quibble,
so you know,
I curse you, God.
And if you want to do something about it,
you know where I live.

TREE

The last thing she saw before her eyes were closed
by the bark that had already sealed her mouth
was a part of the forest, a piece of the sky
she took with her into her silence
and that keeps on growing inside her,
makes her reach higher and higher
as if she could speak from the tip of her top,
as if she could sing.

HER TAIL

It follows after, qualifying;
a piece of punctuation unintentionally ironic.

HER HANDS

Everything is finished in the pristine house
and nothing matters any more but this –

the scrubbed bath, the bowl
filled with bleach, bare silence and

all the windows open for the wind's speech.

THE PAINTER

Though I no longer hold a brush
the sky still spreads its canvas,
that tree is still rising
to its crown, drawing towards it
the shades of evening,
holding heat into the night.

And the river still shines its silver
beneath low-moving cloud
– a fleet of ships
or migrant crowd –
throwing light and shadow
on water, glass and stone.

How changeable it is,
how incomplete. I learn
to begin again: the pale blue
of morning, the inkwell of night,
rain scratching the surface,
leaving no scars.

Twilight's yellows and golds
on an insignificant wall,
the local colour
on a wrist,
on that girl's blouse,
on that man's shirt,

and how the street
leads us through the frame
of its composition.

THE LINE

> *(after Tàpies)*

He's scratched a line from one end to the other
of this sand-covered, landscape-shaped canvas.
The line is thick, a fringe of sand furring its sides,

but there's a crack near the bottom of the picture
as if the whole thing's about to blow wide –
like a flaw in china – the painting's broken.

The thing is, you're not allowed to touch,
although you want to, this surface of a workshop floor
raised to a wall. To touch it feels like what it's for

but please don't touch it. Because of the crack,
the flaw, because it's art, because you want to.
The whole thing might come crashing to the floor.

The whole thing balances as if on an edge.
And this line that seems too wide, a stretching horizon,
is just a line, a heel flaring a sandy floor.

SEA BALLAD

It was more, more than I could bear,
the light on the harbour water,
light dancing through your hair

and the water was dancing
and our dreams went down to the sea
under the iron bridge,
under our constancy

and our dreams, our dreams were dancing,
wildering on the waves
there where the headland and the river
rage

and the wind, the wind was dancing
combing the grass of your hair
where our love went dancing, dancing
out of sight.

There where a tanker passed
as slow as a terrible thought
and a boat perched on its mooring
and strained as wildly as a horse

by the yellow of the sand,
by the yellow of the sea
where our love went dancing, dancing
and you danced away from me.

Although your nightly echo comes
about the corners of the room
in all the languages of man
and all the looks that loving might engender,

and though love has nearly always been a fool
and I have craved it, just a gram,
like a wrap of truffles or cocaine,
I am through with it, and you,
your rule,
your slam, and *shtick*, and cool.

SNOW AT THE WINDOW

The snow seems like something a man mid-stumble
bearing a box of shells and stones

might fling, making suddenly unknown
where any stone or shell might go

and trying, even now, mid-fall, to fumble
each spinning flake of white, each pale tone,

back into its box, the way that I disown,
or try to, everything but snow at the window.

Everything is about to alter and to be different
again: the rain to pass, that age

into this.
                   The mower

nudges one long stem
aquiver. See, everything

is already different from how it is.

LEAVING THE CITY

Shadows fall away
and the City is exposed
as posture and imposture
while the grey of a misty river,

the blue of a misty sky,
collude with our pretence
that we are suspended
like a magician's assistant in the air,

but it is only a temporary
levitation, a giddy trick
of rails, this dawn floatation, this slide
between bank and bank,

as we leave the institutional havoc
where no-one is to blame,
certainly not the boys and girls
in white pumps on the trading floor,

polished Oxfords, and thin-laced brogues.
So soon the City leaves us
and we are taken in
by a volley of glimpses –

shop storerooms, an accountant's office,
a kung-fu hall –
the glazed and the dim
through a patina of grime;

bracketed satellite dishes,
ads for low-paid jobs.
Men in high-viz jackets
stand back to watch us pass,

hands dropped, expressions bored;
we pass a field of cows,
a graffitied bridge, a solitary horse.
The commuter belt arrives

with fences and long gardens,
DIY stores and the little
colourful cars moving to and fro
like tropical fish in a tank

but we are moving faster
through the shoals of trees,
the reefs of gorse. Who knows where
we are aiming, who knows where

we will fall, travelling faster
through a blur of cuttings,
a landscaped golf course, but longing
for the sea and its beginning.

It slumps clothes on the washing line,
opens rings on the boating lake
while under the cafe canopy
figures continue to dance:
forget me, forget-me-not,
do not, do not forget me quite.

THE VALLEY, RAIN COMING

A shock of birds from tall woods scatters like rain over the field,
pivots on nothing, hurls back like leaves before the wind
so madly that you duck and when you stand
you're alone again by the empty woods.

DOWN THE VALLEY, WATER

Churn, charge, ruffle, ripple,
slide, slip, drain, trickle,
puddle, piddle, pour, rush,
maunder, wander, madden, middle,
caper, saunter, canter, spatter,
swirl, sweep, spin, spool,
spurt, jump, lie, lock,
lap, lope, slacken, sigh,
straggle, rumble, splash, cuff –
all down the valley
the water makes its push.

THE TOKEN

'Let me in, let me in,
the woods are broken and all I have
is this plastic yellow token
I found in my pocket when I woke.

I am lost in the wild wood.
Show me which way to go
by fallen trunk, by ivy, and broken stump.
I know my way only by this plastic token
that would feed a slot in a city but, broken,

whatever machine it fed would not take it.
This is hardly something that could be spoken
but I am lost in the wild wood
and my time is broken.'

THE HOUSE

Beyond the woods
stands a house by a bridge
grown up thick with sedge.
In spring the floods
devour its edge.

Beyond the woods
stands a house by a bridge.

Whatever you have of goods
not kept on a high ledge
floats out to the last hedge.

Beyond the woods
stands a house by a bridge
grown up thick with sedge.

The heart does not let go
easily its desires.
The heart has many fires.
It eats up so
many epics in its funeral pyres,
the heart does not let go
easily its desires.

It leaps up slow
and fast, it tires,
it burns whole quires.

The heart does not let go
easily its desires.
The heart has many fires.

Perhaps I could count for you the animals,
the skinny fox, the frightened deer, the pony
with the pot-belly that blocks my path
some mornings, oblivious,
all the neighbourhood's elusive strays.

Or perhaps I could count for you the birds,
the heron in the tree, as still as a spear,
the scrawny blackbird in his tattered coat
or else the heartbeat of the kingfisher
you would fit inside your gentle fist.

Or perhaps I could count for you the ghosts
that rise each morning to take their place
on the banks of the fens, old drowned grey ones
as quiet as herons or strays; I hear them whispering
in the dawn, of your good, and things past.

A-ROAD

The ones who walk at night alone, along
the dual carriageway's thin margin
in sopping trainers past heavy freight,
the ones who missed their bus or lift,
the ones we read about in Sunday papers,
the ones who saw the yellow leaves,
fat ruby rings in Christmas crackers,
who listened to the whoosh and whump
and spray of passing traffic, the ones
who dreamed they'd find a turquoise bay,
its waters as smooth as fresh-ironed sheets,
its houses as perfect as a doll's perfect house –
to them, this A-road is the long road home.

MARSH SONGS

Where the lane comes down to the crossing
past cows and butterflies, it comes to nothing.

*

The world gets lost out here, where things
turn shapes, and shapes turn doors   into the mist.

*

The mist takes everything away but the yellow
irises in June, butterflies, electric-blue dragonflies.

*

The air's ice, joints stiff, the web of flesh
between thumb and finger aches; it hurts to make a fist.

*

What would you say, my love, to this:
slushy crystals sliding the windscreen, sun-kissed?

*

Cows at the marsh edge flummox, chew, brood
in their Buddhist robes by the flowered hedge.

THE WIND

Coming up the estuary over the nameless places
by the long muddy reaches of the sea
– an archery range, a caravan park, a tiny beach,
an installation of silver pipes and chimneys
shining as brightly as love might do at dusk –
the wind almost says their names,
coming up the river, rubbing everything away.

Men play snooker in the clubhouse gloom.
A cue ball clacks. Behind the bar, light glows.
A golfball pitches on the eighteenth green.
Waves are ripping up the shore again, again, again.

SUNDAY AFTERNOON

Spray on the pier, a curved slash of beach –
it's the hour of the dog, the hour of regret,
the hour of promises – and promises
you'll break, break-ups, break-downs, lost love.

A quiet hour when a tap drips, a couple walk
uncertainly hand in hand. Fists in pockets,
fishermen stand by angled rods. It's the hour
when rain coaxes the streets into forgetting,

and finally, still raining, it's dusk.

SLEEPLESS

Not the breaking, the grief,
the act of being broken,
but – gentle, gentle – the rain
falling on the roofs, the grass, the sea.

ISLAND

On an archipelago, believe in the rocks.
They seem to be numbered like the stars,
the sea confounded by voyages of loss.

Gulls meditate on entrails, pink worms in grass,
the dead hand of a crab on a stone as green as moss.
On an archipelago, believe in the rocks.

Wet weather moves in, the sun dissolves;
she wears rags of rain, a smoky wedding dress;
the sea is confounded by these voyages of loss.

The ships go by, frowning on their course,
not so much vanished as forgotten;
on an archipelago, believe in the rocks.

The village with its cobbled square is locked
and from each greeny cliff a derelict pillbox
confronts the sea's long voyages of loss.

Birds hang in the wind, clutch at twigs. They're cold.
Snow mounts small campaigns in corners of a field.
On an archipelago, believe in the rocks.
The sea is confounded by voyages of loss.

SONNET

The Winter Gardens, of course, are closed –
an unbroken acre of grille-covered glass.
Modelled on a church, each apse is short,

the tower edged with electric bulbs,
and every one is blown.
Each petal-cornered wrought-iron arch

spans a gap of daylit air.
Disused beside a bowling alley,
the coin judder of arcades.

But, in echoing the body of a church
– its ribs, its skin of glass – it echoes too
a ship, beyond that, the human form,

a naked man lying on his back, open
to sun, mist, hail, a summer storm.

RICHARD LAMBERT was born in London in 1971. He did a PhD in medieval history at the University of Bristol on stories from medieval Paris about landscapes in northern France. His poetry pamphlet *The Magnolia* was published in 2008 and his poetry collection *Night Journey* was published in 2012.

In fiction, Richard graduated from the MA in Creative Writing at UEA with a distinction. His short story *The Hazel Twig and the Olive Tree* was shortisted for the 2017 Sunday Times EFG Short Story Award, and he was a runner-up in the Bridport Prize for his short story *Turtles*.

He has worked in higher education, local government, and the NHS, and is an experienced creative writing tutor. He lives in Norwich.